The Gardens of Villandry

Executive editor
Catherine Laulhère-Vigneau

Design and layout
Laurent Picard & Estève Gili

English translation
Alexander Fyjis-Walker

Engraver
Sele Offset Torino/ Italy

Photographs
© Jean-Baptiste Leroux / Hoaqui
P. 137 © Lavaud/Photothèque de Villandry

© Éditions Plume, 1998
2 rue de la Roquette - 75011 Paris

ISBN 2 84110 099 5

The Gardens of Villandry

Robert and Henri Carvallo   —   Jean-Baptiste Leroux

EDITIONS PLUME

For my parents, Marguerite and Robert Carvallo,
who taught me to see beauty, and gave me the
strength to make Villandry live.

Henri Carvallo

Contents

History and architecture

Fifteen kilometres west of Tours, and nine west of Azay-le-Rideau, Villandry, built in 1536, is the last in the series of the great Renaissance châteaux of the Loire. It was the seat neither of a king, nor of a king's mistress, but of one of François I's ministers, Jean Le Breton (whose family seems to have hailed, the name notwithstanding, from Scotland). Le Breton's calling might have been as a financier, but his architectural experience was considerable. For many years his work for the Crown included overseeing and directing the construction of Chambord, near which he built a scaled down version of Villandry, Villesavin. Earlier in his career he had been an ambassador in Italy where he had had the opportunity to study the art of gardening. His creation, Villandry, has been hardly marked by the dramas of French history, tragic or comic, and the reason is that Le Breton, more honest or more cunning than the other great builders of his time, was never disgraced, nor had his goods seized and his château appropriated, as were Chenonceau or Azay, by the Crown. It is not for its history that the visitor will make pilgrimage to Villandry, but for the harmonious vision of architecture and gardens perfectly integrated in their natural surroundings. Working now on his own account, Jean Le Breton allowed himself to experiment with new ideas.

An old feudal fortress stood on the site, and this he demolished down to the foundations, with the exception of the south-west keep, scene of the dramatic encounter on 4 July 1189 when Henry II of England came, two days before his death, to acknowledge defeat in the presence of Philippe Auguste. Jean Le Breton incorporated this keep into the three ranges of the new château, built in an apparently very simple style, and forming a U-shape opening to a grand panorama of the valley through which flow the Cher and the Loire.

Arcaded galleries, windows with richly stuccoed surrounds, tall and shapely dormers, grandiose slate roofs running at precipitous angles, all serve to frame a *cour d'honneur* of exceptionally elegant proportions. The monotony that often repels the eye when symmetry is too rigidly the principle of a building is banished by the discreet use of a panoply of architectural sleights-of-hand: the reflection of the façades in the moat, the slight irregularity in the angles between the ranges, the subtle difference in length of the different ranges, the way the principal windows are placed slightly off centre, the calculated play of shadows changing throughout the day... The Château and gardens are at their most beautiful two hours before sunset. For all that Villandry is near Azay-le-Rideau both in space and time, Italian influences and medieval echoes - turrets, clock-towers, decorative crenellation - have entirely disappeared, making way to a simpler, purely French style that, especially in the design of the roofs, prefigures Anet, Fontainebleau and what will come to be called the Henri IV style. Yet Villandry's originality lies not just in an avant-garde view of architecture, but also in the way the site has been used in the layout of gardens of exceptional beauty, fully in harmony with the stone and landscape of the Loire valley. These gardens were designed and laid out between 1907 and 1920 by a Spanish doctor, Joachim Carvallo, drawing his inspiration both from local tradition and the remains of the original layout, which had been destroyed in the 18th century.

The west façade of the château, which has recently been restored: the entrance courtyard and the cour d'honneur

Joachim Carvallo and the Gardens of Villandry

At first glance, there was nothing to mark Joachim Carvallo out as the future creator of the gardens of Villandry and the founder of the *Demeure Historique*. He was born in 1869 in Don Benito, a large market town in Extremadura, unquestionably Spain's most austere province. His father had set up there in a small way as a miller and a distiller of aniseed, but died young, leaving his wife to educate three small children with very reduced means. Life cannot always have been easy for them in Don Benito.

The eldest, a girl, became a nun, the youngest, a boy, became a journalist, and Joachim Carvallo went to Madrid to study medicine. His brilliance can be measured by the fact that he was allowed to finish his studies at the then world-renowned Faculty of Medicine in Paris. There he became the favourite pupil of Professor Charles Richet (who was to win the Nobel Prize in 1913), and met his future wife, Ann Coleman. She was a scientist like him, original like him, and like him drawn to Paris by the fame of the university. They fell in love and their plans for marriage were given decisive support by Professor Richet, who undertook to go to America to persuade the bride's family, who were Protestant, well-off, traditionally minded and not a little reluctant to give their consent. Around 1906, the Carvallos had the idea of buying a large country house with space enough for their laboratories, and where they could carry out their joint research in comfort. This house was Villandry, and the move was a turning point in their lives. Villandry at the time, disfigured by 18th and 19th century alterations, was a large barracks surrounded by a dreary garden in the English style. What it was that triggered, a year after their arrival, a revelation to Joachim Carvallo of the hidden magic of the place, we shall never know. But it fired him to pour all his energy and passion into bringing its beauty back to life. From that moment on he completely abandoned his career and his scientific ambitions.

As far as the château is concerned, Joachim Carvallo's was a work of restoration, generally agreed to be brilliantly successful. The gardens, on the other hand, are far more than that. He had no archive material to work from, such as a plan of the gardens before they were taken down to make the English park.

The only evidence was archaeological, in particular buried walls that showed how the gentle slopes of the English garden had been laid out over a set of terraces arranged over three levels, whose layout soon emerged with some clarity. Working from this information, Joachim Carvallo set out to read every word that had been printed on the subject of old gardens. This research led him, in particular, to the monastic library at Solesmes. He must have been very greatly in thrall to his new passion, for his numerous contacts with the Benedictines at that abbey, together with his musings on the sources of our civilization, acted in such a way that in around 1910 he converted from radical agnosticism to a Catholicism that was both mystical and inflexible. Indeed the religious element was very important to his creation, as he revealed in an article written in 1924: 'Art proceeds from a long contemplation of nature by which the human spirit penetrates the intimate essence of things, feels their poetry, and in a supreme effort lifts itself to God.' All in all, if the gardens at Villandry are inspired by historical example, they are far from being a simple reconstruction. They are the original work of a man of our century. Enough time has elapsed since they were made for us to be able to appreciate how exceptional the quality of his work is.

Joachim Carvallo, creator of the gardens at Villandry, and his American wife Ann Coleman

The castle and the gardens as they were in 1906, before Joachim Carvallo embarked on his project of restoring the castle to its Renaissance purity and to create gardens in harmony with it

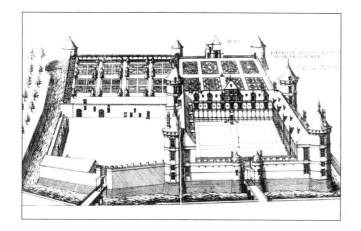

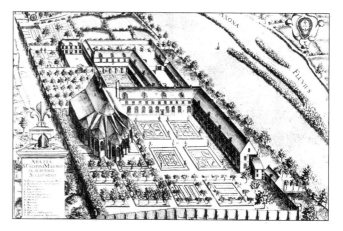

The two source books that inspired Joachim Carvallo : the Monasticon Gallicanum and The most Excellent Buildings of France by Androuet du Cerceau. This drawing shows the château of Bury, where the organizing principle of the gardens and the castle is comparable to the design carried out at Villandry

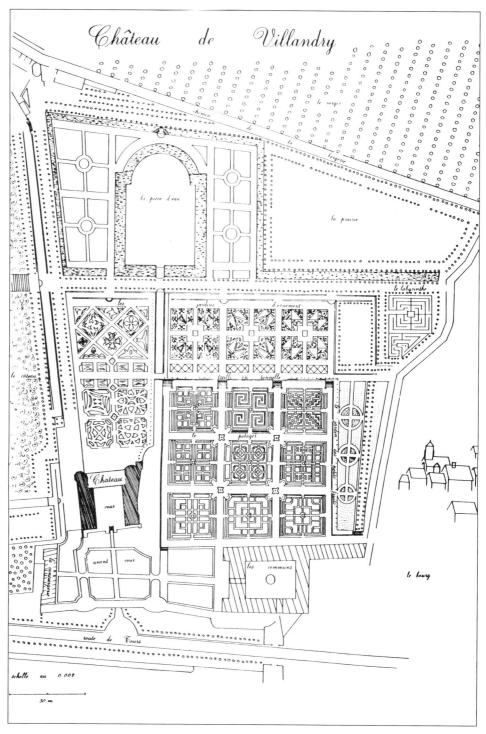

Plan of the gardens at Villandry as they are today

The layout of the gardens

A little valley with a stream running through it descends from the plateau to the south of the château. Thanks to the slope, the gardens can be laid out in three levels of terracing.

At the highest level is a large basin, shaped like a Louis XV mirror and known as *le miroir d'eau*; its water is used to feed the moat, the fountains, and the irrigation systems. In the middle, on the same level as the public rooms of the château, is a *jardin d'ornement* - an ornamental or pleasure garden - with flower beds framed by box hedges.

And finally, under the windows of the west wing and on the same level as the outbuildings, is the third and most original of the three gardens: the ornamental kitchen garden.

Each of these three gardens is surrounded and overlooked by a raised and covered pathway (a limetree-vaulted pergola on the top level, grapevines trailing over a trellis below). Thus the visitor is able to wander at his ease to examine the gardens, protected from the heat of the sun. The principle is that enunciated by Olivier de Serres: 'It is desirable for gardens to be viewed from above, either from contiguous buildings, or from raised terraces surrounding the beds.' In addition, all three gardens are protected by the setting. To the east, stand the château and the upper terraces. These are cut out of the flank of a leafy hill that rises fully fifty metres above the garden. To the west are the village and ancient church, which face the château from the other side of the little valley and dominate the kitchen garden. As in the Middle Ages, neither village nor church has been thrust aside by the great house, as was to be common practice from the beginning of the 17th century.

To the north are the outbuildings: stables and cowsheds whose high walls deflect all the coldest winds from the kitchen garden. And to the south, the gardens run into open countryside. A large orchard rises gently in a natural transition towards the fields on the plateau. Thus all is arranged at Villandry so that a small space constantly overlooked by the inhabitants of the château can provide all that is needful for material as well as spiritual well-being.

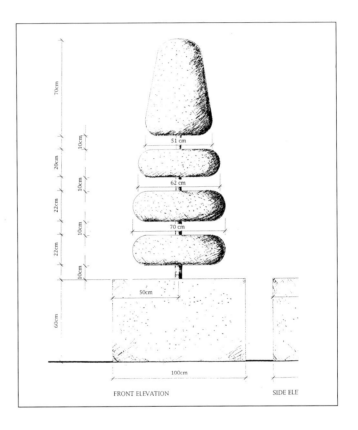

FRONT ELEVATION   SIDE ELE

The topiary (box, lime, yew) is currently being restored. Sixty yew trees in the traditional Villandry shape were replaced in 1997 and 1998. Right: the gardens are laid out over three levels of terracing: the kitchen garden, the jardin d'ornement, and the water garden. On the same level as the jardin d'ornement is the physic garden, completing the functional value of the kitchen garden

Gardening techniques

In total, the gardens at Villandry cover five hectares. They are looked after by a team of nine full time gardeners, and it is their dedication to the task that makes Villandry what it is. Nevertheless, the ratio of nine gardeners to five hectares is relatively low, considering the density of planting. Consequently, strong motivation and a love of the job are essential. To be able to work in such an exceptional place might be motivation enough, but in addition the work is very varied, and there are opportunities to use the most modern horticultural techniques; moreover the pay is excellent.

A precisely organized timetable, and rigorous planning are vital. I can illustrate the last point with the example of the planting arrangements which have to be prepared each year for the kitchen garden.

This is a complex task that takes many hours to complete, and requires the participation of the whole gardening team. Two plans are needed every year. The spring plan uses the following vegetables: peas, broad beans, radishes, lentils, spring cabbage, lettuces (romaine, red and green oak-leaves, 'Reine de mai', batavia, salad bowl and red salad bowl).

Some perennials are also included: strawberries, sorrel, chives. These remain in place for up to four or five years. To bring some colour to the kitchen garden, various spring flowers are planted in the edging of each *carré*: alternating red and yellow pansies, large white daisies, blue pansies, forget-me-nots, stock. These biennials are planted out in the previous autumn.

The summer plan fixes the arrangement of flowers and vegetables from June into autumn. The main vegetables used are: 'Autoro' cabbages, 'Pigeon' ornamental cabbages, green with a red heart, 'Peacock' ornamental cabbages, green with a white heart, early 'hâtifs de Vienne' cabbages, Savoy cabbages, pumpkins, spinach beet and Swiss chard, golden celery, celeriac, carrots, Bleus de Solaise leeks, aubergines, capsicums, tomatoes, chives, parsley, basil, round or long beetroot, gourds, endives, cardoons. The edgings of the *carrés* are given a summer livery of annuals: petunias, verbena, purple sage, marigold, begonias, tobacco plants. Altogether the kitchen garden uses some twenty thousand flowering plants, sixty thousand vegetables in spring and forty thousand in summer, making a total for both seasons of a hundred and twenty thousand plants.

Each planting has to take account of factors both technical and aesthetic:

The technical factors: Crop rotation

It is not a good idea, for example, to plant carrots in a bed used the previous year for celery, since both vegetables belong to the Umbellifer family and so take the same nutrients from the soil and are vulnerable to the same soil-borne diseases. In the same way cabbages and radishes, both Crucifers, should not be allowed to follow each other. Thus careful crop rotation is essential if soil exhaustion and plant disease are to be avoided. To give an idea of the complexity of the problem: there are eight botanical families; it is advisable to wait three years before replanting a bed with a member of the same family. And at Villandry there are two plantings a year for each bed!

The aesthetic factors: combining colour and form

The patterning of colour and forms is the second major factor in planning the kitchen garden plantings. It's a demanding problem, since vegetables generally offer little in the way of colour contrast. For example, capsicums and tomatoes should not be placed side by side, since their leaves are very similar in hue. We try instead to try to bring together contrasts such as the jade green of carrots and the blue of the Solaise leeks, or the red of beetroot leaves and the golden-tinted green of celery. Tall vegetables, like aubergines and artichokes, need to be shown near low plants like lettuce or sorrel.

The photographs in the last chapter of this book show the results of our gardeners' art.

Planting out
the biennials
(here, forget-me-nots)
in autumn

Villandry today

Built of luminously beautiful but fragile stone, Villandry needs a fortune for its upkeep. Joachim Carvallo happily sacrificed that of his wife to the stately home and garden. Today, his family depend on the admission charge to maintain the château and the gardens: a task that occupies a workforce of twenty and uses an annual budget for upkeep and major works of some eight million francs. In 1997, 350,000 visitors came to Villandry, compared to the 50,000 who came in 1971, too few to pay for proper maintenance. Over the same period, the number of gardeners has leapt from four to nine. Villandry now finds itself in a virtuous circle whose essential elements are the quality of the upkeep of the gardens and the scale of the major restoration projects. Visitors quickly appreciate the work and improvements and spread the word; their friends come; each year visitor numbers rise and so each year we can enlarge the scope of our restoration projects. The marketing budget at Villandry is very small by the standards of comparable tourist attractions; we rely on word of mouth.

To fulfil our ambition that the garden should be a thing of beauty for our visitors requires enormous discipline. In a place where the building stone is so delicate and where the geometry of the gardens can allow of no imperfection, beauty can come about only as a result of unremitting hard work and constant supervision. Running Villandry is like running a small business, with the difference that the goal is not to make profits but constantly to improve this unique site.

The four carrés of the Garden of Love, whose layout is inspired by the gardens of Moorish Spain

The kitchen garden

The kitchen garden

●

Villandry's kitchen garden covers a hectare, and consists of nine *carrés*, the square beds so popular in France during the Renaissance. Each of these is identical in size but with a different box hedge pattern Inside these hedges forty-odd varieties of vegetables and flowers are planted out, their alternating colours making up a rainbow chequerboard. Each year sees two plantings, one in the spring (March to June) and the other in summer (July to October). The kitchen garden was reconstructed at the beginning of this century by Joachim Carvallo, who drew his inspiration from the classic kitchen gardens of the Renaissance, recorded by Androuet de Cerceau in his book *The Most Excellent Buildings of France*. The decorative kitchen garden of the Renaissance descends from the monastic traditions of the Middle Ages, enhanced in the 16th century by decorative elements imported from Italy, such as arbours, fountains and flower beds.

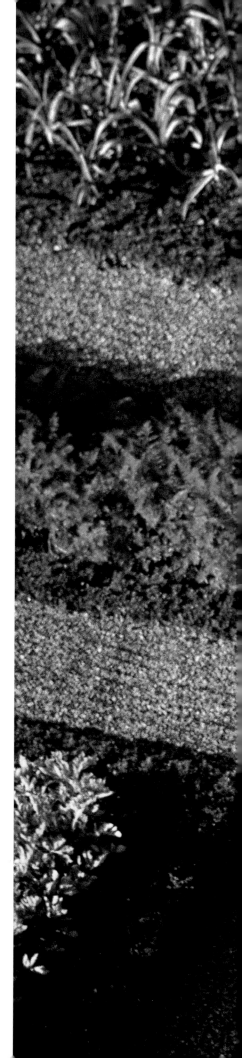

Aerial view of the kitchen garden: the numerous crosses recall the monastic origins of its design

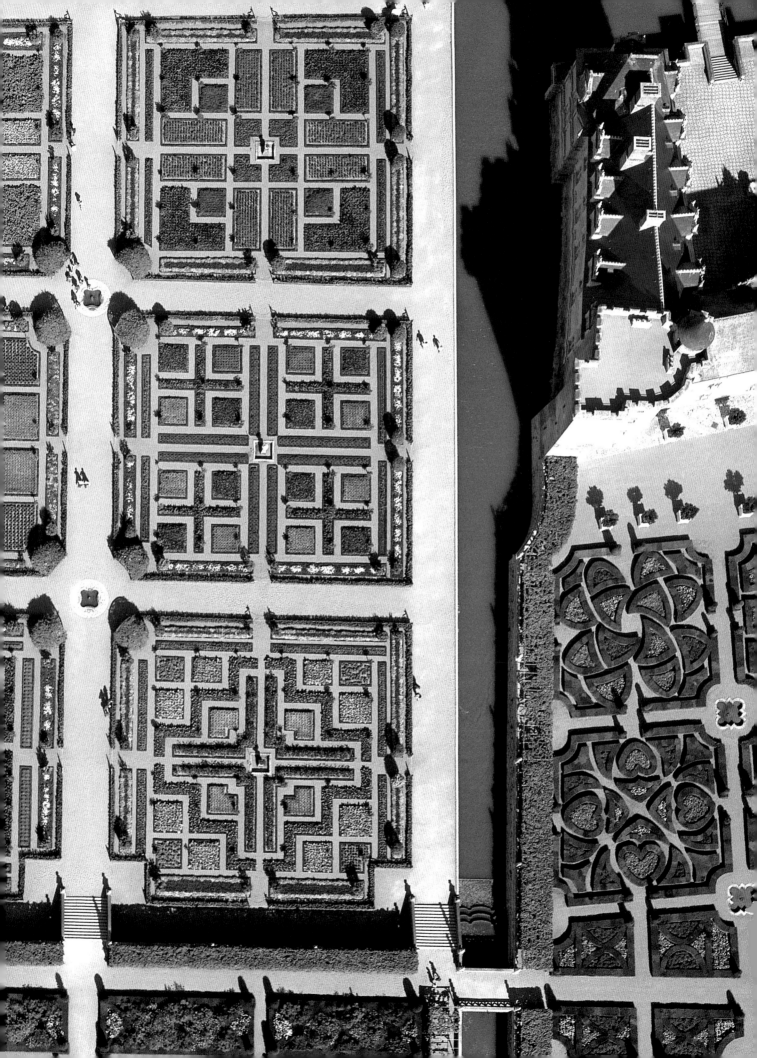

Left: The red beet, one of the beautiful vegetables that adorn the kitchen garden in summer

Right: a path in the woods rises almost fifty metres above the kitchen garden: a fine bird's eye view

Vegetables in the
kitchen garden are
interspersed with
flowers and fruit:
each of the squares
has thirty standard
roses, laid out in
geometric patterns,
and sixteen pyramid-
trained pear-trees

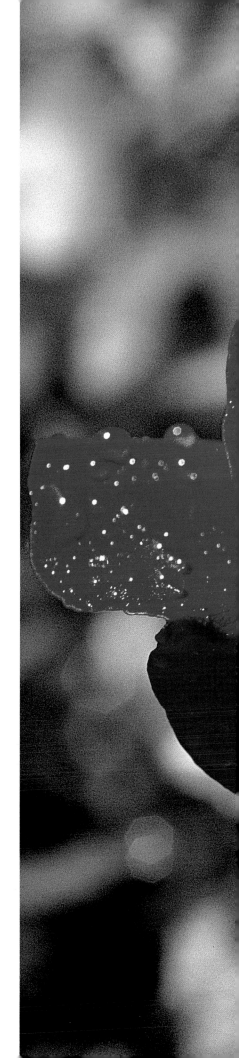

The texture,
form and colour of
each vegetable all
contribute to the
multicoloured
chequerboard a
of the kitchen garden

Left:
detail of a leek

Right:
detail of a capsicum

Following pages:
red beet and golden celery

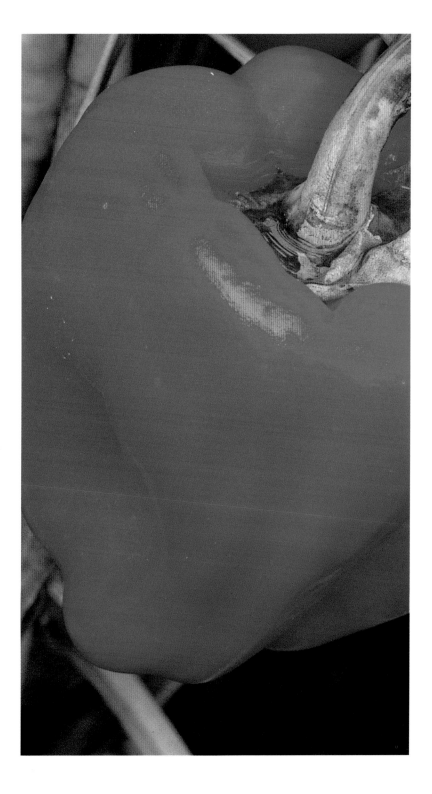

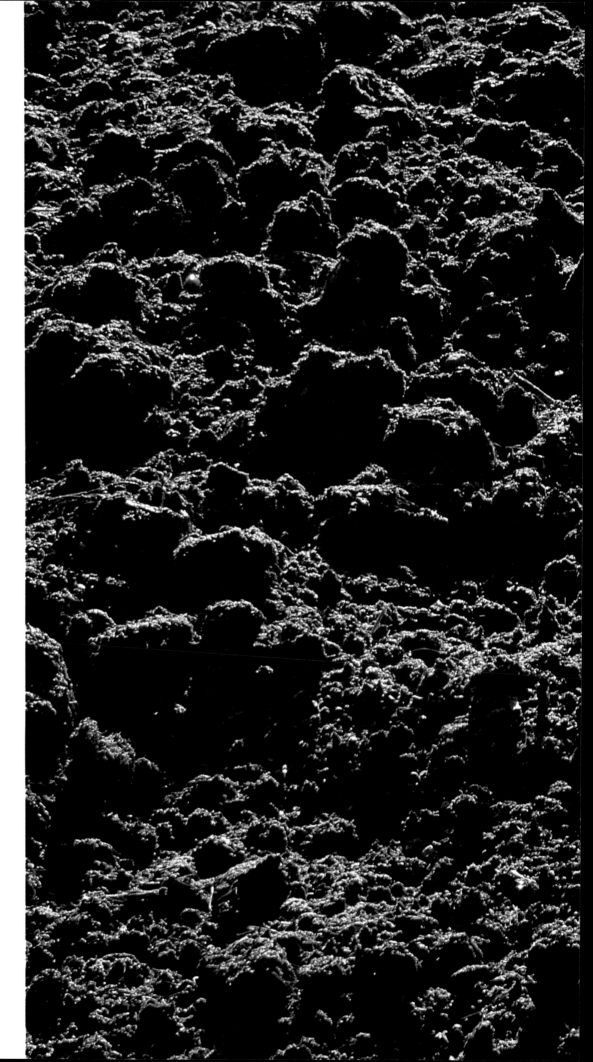

The soil in the kitchen garden is very rich. Its physical and chemical qualities are carefully monitored by Patrick Chaudoy, the head gardener

Left: A raised walk, shaded by an arbour, runs round the kitchen garden, so that it can be enjoyed even in the hot summer sun

Right: a sturdy romanesque church overlooks the gardens of Villandry, a constant reminder of heavenly things in this earthly paradise

The kitchen garden was originally watered from the fountain in the middle of each square; an automatic irrigation system is now used to water all five hectares

Clumps of flowers
brighten the squares
of the kitchen garden.
Here, begonias and
cineraria, red tobacco-
plants and ageratum

An important element in
the kitchen garden
is the Loire gravel
(*mignonette*) used
on the paths, raked into
patterns that reinforce
the rigorous geometry of
the gardens

Left and overleaf:
The arched bowers
covered in roses
and honeysuckle and
the fountains all attest to
the Italian influence
that brought a new
liveliness to the medieval
monastic gardens
(also overleaf)

Some of the
summer vegetables:
pumpkin, decorative
cabbage, red tomatoes

Salads make up
most of the spring
crops; their regular
habit allows
very exact patterns
to be laid out

The layout of
the gardens appears
in all its purity
under the snow

Following pages:
sunrise over the three main
buildings of Villandry:
church, château,
and outbuildings

The steps from
the kitchen garden to
the jardin d'ornement

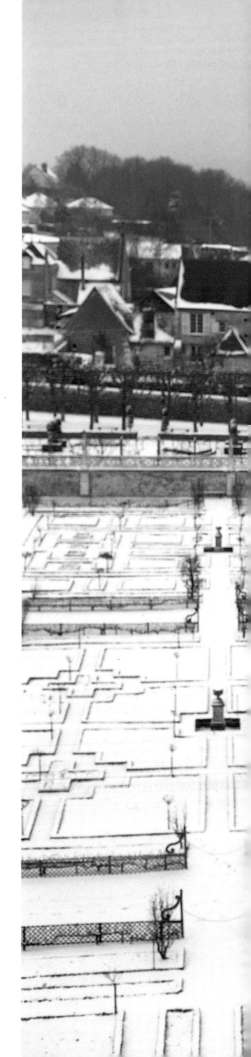

The jardin d'ornement

•

The jardin d'ornement

•

The *jardin d'ornement* − ornemental garden or pleasure garden − are the outside drawing rooms of the château. Situated on the middle terrace, above the kitchen garden and on the same level as the reception rooms inside the château, it consists of box parterres, punctuated by clipped yew trees and filled with flowers. This garden was designed by Lozano, a Sevillian artist and friend of Joachim Carvallo, who found his inspiration in the gardening art of the Spanish Moors. There are two sections; (also called salons − drawing rooms) in the first, to the south of the château, a symbolic picture of the progress of love is shown in four squares: inconstancy, tenderness, passion, tragedy. The design of this first section is rounded off with squares showing the Maltese, Languedoc and Basque crosses. The second *salon*, west of the moats, is the Garden of Music.

*The Garden of Love,
seen from
the castle windows*

In April, the tulips in
the jardin d'ornement
are in flower,
and punctuate
the blue carpet of
forget-me-nots

*Detail from the
Garden of Love:
in the middle of the
hearts, mask shapes
suggest the romance
of masked balls*

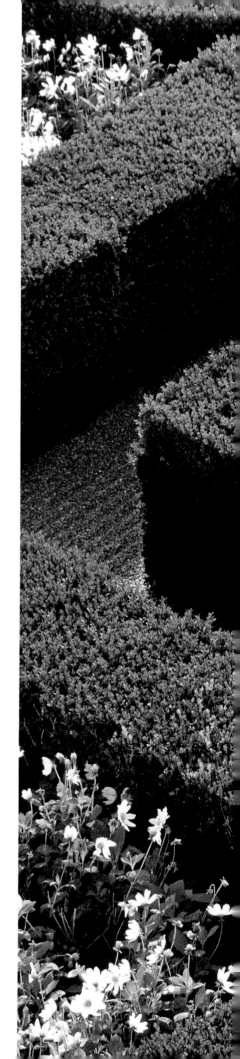

The squares of the Garden of Love lead into the Garden of the Crosses. Here, the Basque Cross

Left: *forget-me-nots*
and tulips lend
colour to the hearts
in the Garden of Love

One of the monumental
fountains that
survive from the
eighteenth-century garden

In the background,
the Maltese Cross

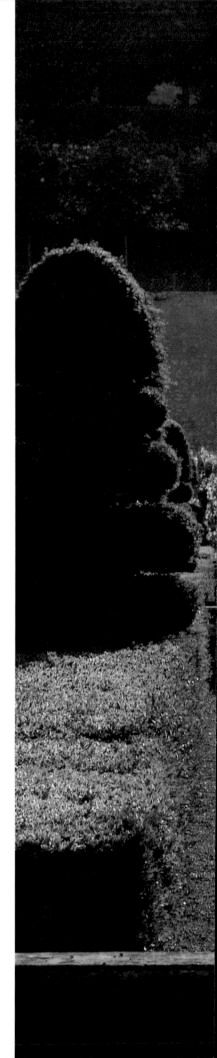

The Garden of Music,
to the west of the château

In summer the forget-
me-nots and tulips
are replaced by dahlias

In September,
asters in the
Garden of Music

Right: the carrés
of the Garden of
Love in summer:
four varieties of
dahlias are used

The Garden of Music,
seen from the hill that
overlooks the garden

A subtle colouring
is achieved by the
perennials: lavander
and sea-lavender

A series of terraces looks out over the jardin d'ornement, giving a bird's eye view that enables its geometry to be fully appreciated

One of the fountains in
the Garden of Music

Left: Inconstant
love in winter,
summer and spring.
Lower right,
passionate love

The fountains of the
Garden of Love
recall those in
the Moorish gardens
of Granada

The water garden

•

The water garden

•

On the upper level is a large basin in the shape of a Louis XV mirror, called *le miroir*. It is the centrepiece of a classic garden in the French style, set in a green amphitheatre, whose pure and sober lines lead to a sense of calm and meditation.

As well as being ornamental, this basin also has a vital function, providing the waters that feed both the watering systems and all the fountains.

The basin glistens like a Louis XV mirror

*The calm waters
of this great
basin have been
home to several
generations of swans*

Ball-clipped box trees
in square planters
give sculptural interest
to the water garden

The fountains at
Villandry play an
important role,
bringing music
to the gardens with
the gentle plashing
of water on stone, and
lending a freshness
to the summer air

A series of cascades carries the waters of the basin down to the moats

Details of the cascades on the north-south canal

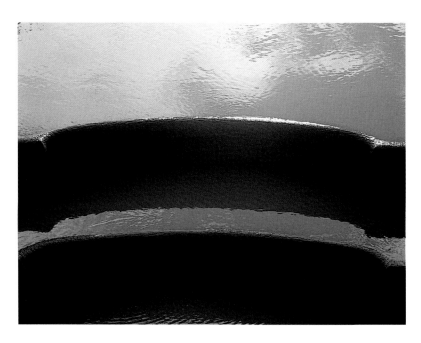

*Running from
north to south,
this canal constitutes
of the principal
axes of the garden*

The
gardening
year

The gardening year

The great diversity of the gardens at Villandry, and the various kinds of work required depending on the season, mean that a large number of different horticultural techniques are used here. The gardening team need all of their wide range of skills.

The main stages of the gardening year are:

● Spring: in March, the spring crops are planted out in the kitchen garden. In June, these are harvested and immediately replaced by the summer planting. Dahlias are planted out in the *jardin d'ornement*. First clipping of the box hedges and the yews.

● Summer: Upkeep (weeding), clipping the hornbeam hedges, sowing the biennials under glass.

● Autumn: planting tulips and forget-me-nots; harvesting the vegetables and clearing the summer flowers, maintaining the woods, second clipping of the box hedges and the yews.

● Winter: pruning the limes, fruit-trees and vines. Sowing the summer flowers under glass. Carrying on the rolling programme of replacing the topiary (yews, limes, box).

*Mid-March:
the spring vegetables
are planted out
in the kitchen garden
over a single week*

Left:
*hoeing the
lettuces in April*

Top right:
*the lettuces a month
after planting out*

Middle right:
*the lawns
are mown two to
three times a week
during the spring*

Bottom right:
the gardening team

If the lawns around
the basin are
to be in optimum
condition, they need
to be relaid regularly.
This task is carried
out in the spring

The whole garden
is served by an
automatic
watering system,
in daily use
during the summer

The yews are
clipped in July

In summer,
strimmers are
needed to clear out
around the trees

The paths in the
kitchen garden
can only be weeded
with a hoe,
as the box hedges
are too delicate
for weedkillers
to be used

In autumn the
biennials (here
forget-me-nots)
are planted
out in the jardin
d'ornement

Vegetables are
harvested
gradually in
the kitchen garden
from October on

Right hand page:
white beets
and ornamental
cabbages
are left until
the first frosts

The lime-tree leaves
are gathered up
every day
in the autumn

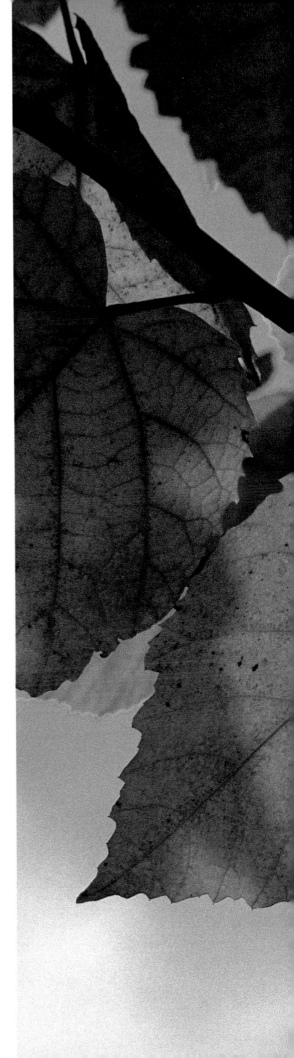

A blower is
used to gather
dead leaves

Right hand page:
Robert Carvallo,
grandson of
Joachim, and his wife
Marguerite
d'Estienne d'Orves,
planning out the
kitchen garden,
an autumn task.
The unfailing
dedication with
which Robert and
Marguerite Carvallo
laboured at Villandry
laid the foundations
of the château's
tourist success and
created the means
to carry out a large-
scale programme
of major restoration

Pruning the
1260 lime trees
occupies four
gardeners
for two months.
The mobile platform
and power shears
have made
the job quicker
and easier

*Apple trees in
the kitchen garden
being traimed
in February*

Printed in Spain

D.L. TO: 185-1999